A refuge, a mother, and a depository of all our sins.

The sea lives on, while empires and civilisations rise and fall.

The lessons we can learn from it are infinite.

Sand

I generally try to keep a low profile.
I was never one to become fixated with my identity.

It is true, I may consist of leftover scraps,
crumbs of half-eaten civilisations long perished,
But make no mistake:
I am powerful.
I am immortal.
I can become anything I want,
and I can survive the harshest conditions.

So look out for me if you want to learn about your past.
because I befriend conflict and chaos.
I thrive where the hammer meets the stone,
where the sea and earth settle their differences.

And I wait,
patiently,
until they have annihilated each other,
because I am all that remains:
I am the destruction, and I am the hope.
The supernova, and the stardust.

Turquoise

At the outer fringes of the cold spectrum,
lies a different kind of colour concoction.

An unlikely sibling within the blue family:
the jovial one.
the glass-full optimist.
A combination of misplaced wavelengths:
the sunny, refreshing juice of a citrus,
squeezed over the aching blue heart of a hopeless poet.

Somehow, you made the combination work.
But although you may be the one
that got away from the gloom,

you never strayed too far.

Salt

Expelled from solution
Hardened by the loneliness
I saw you,
finally uncloaked.

Revealing yourself
in pure white diamonds,
desperate to attract,
Waiting to be tamed by water again
Become brine, sweat and tears again

Abandoning the diamond castle,
for a life in anonymous ubiquity

Crest

They begin their lives humbly, at first.

But soon,
inflated by ambition, they rise.
Foolishly impatient to grow,
to tower over other waves fearlessly,
only to realise that they got ahead of themselves.

Their demise begins at the top:
first, a small crack.
then, a stampede of suicidal avalanches,
tumbling over each other.

The walls that rise the fastest,
are those who break down first,
even before they reach the shore.

Encore

I always felt envious of the sea.

Like an artist prodigy,
she's oblivious to her own talent.

Like a brave revolutionary,
never runs away from her true feelings.

Whether brooding, disturbed or withdrawn,
she always follows the flow of the moment,
unafraid to express what lies below the surface.

And when she needs validation,
she simply applauds herself.

Amplified

It travels hundreds of years
to reach its destination,
only to become reflected.
Deflected.
Rejected.

Light, is a refugee:
Adaptable.
Fearless.
Inventive.

Having fled the war inside the helium core in a hurry,
all it could quickly grab was its warmth.

Unphased by the long journey ahead,
it persists,
eventually falling into the arms of a leaf.
An empty street.
A smile.

To The Ocean

The first time you appeared to me was from afar.
No need to announce yourself.
It was the huge expanse of colour below the horizon
that came ever so much closer as I walked towards you.
It was a deep, solid indigo-violet on that day,
against the blinding yellow sand.
It was the day I met you.

I didn't know
that I would end up growing up on your shores.
On the shallow edge of your vastness.

You allowed me to enter you.
But never said a word to me.
I often wondered why the silence.

Other times you were too angry for me to enter.
All I could do was watch
as you beat yourself up on the shore in agony,
wave after wave after wave.
I wanted to know what made you so angry.
I wanted to help you.

Because you were always there for me.
My amniotic fluid. My go-to refuge.
Someone that always listens.
And doesn't judge.

Red Flag

Today the sea is confused.
It enters the vicious cycle
of rumination and regret,
as the waves beat themselves up on the shore,
and begin to doubt their purpose.

Drowning waves look almost just like normal ones,
until you look much closer,
and you can tell
that they have been distracted:

Poorly formed crests,
incomplete surfs,
like the half-spoken sentences of a PTSD victim:
they are too traumatised to release their energy.

Too tired of the back and forth,
swelling and breaking mechanically,
without passion,
they have began to sense their own futility.

They foolishly thought
that there was something more to THIS.

Regret

Sea storms may be damaging,
but they can inflict much more damage
to the sea itself.

Exhausted from exertion,
torn apart by inner conflict,
the sea is suddenly overtaken by remorse.

Withdrawing into a gentle lake,
it grieves
for the victims of last night's war,
as gentle, barely audible waves,
reach out like hands across the sand,
trying to make amends.

Offering an apology for last night's behaviour,
until the next storm.

Dawn

Like a guilty party reveller,
the light tiptoes its way in slowly,
hoping that it will enter unnoticed.

In a world of on and off switches,
it still prefers to do things the old-fashioned way:

Gradually.
Gracefully.
Compassionately.

Even those who dread a new start,
have the time to change their mind.

About everything.

Cobalt

Sometimes when the light is just right,
it will appear out in the far distance:
just below the horizon,
a faint, yet frigidly pure strip of electric blue,
distilled over and over
through hundreds of miles of atmosphere.

Protected from contamination,
it stays safely in the distance.

Envied by all,
even the rainbow,
a symbol of all the things we can never reach,

the things we cannot even understand.

Reincarnation

Every day,
destruction and rebirth,
as the sea flows into land,
and land flows into sea.

Hoards of new souls,
eager to replace the ones lost in the waves,
like footsteps in the sand erasing one another,
erasing their past,
erased by a wave,
erased by the wind,

Replaced,
Misplaced,
Deconstructed.

Discovered,
Reconstituted,
Re-born.

Like waves,
never wasted,
perpetually reincarnated.

Night

Only when the night returns,
does it become apparent:
That the light, was only a brief interruption,
in an otherwise infinite blackness.

For we are nothing but passengers,
sheltering on a creaking ship.

Surrounded by an endless charcoal desert,
we turn our backs to the blackness,
and face each other.

Navigated by each others' blindness,
we look to faint stars sown into black velvet,
as we ration our hope,
and we wait,
for time

to take its revenge.

Meeting Point

I've seen it in my dreams.
Dead people don't go to heaven.
They all gather on a long beach,
Where all other dead beings go.

Some of them wander about restlessly,
looking for their other dead relatives,
much like seashells on the beach,
eternally looking for their lost half.

This is nature's central morgue:
all bodies are cleansed by the waves,
neatly displayed on the sand like seashells,
gracefully,
patiently,
waiting.

For someone to recognise them,
or simply fancy them,
pick them up,
give them their new life.

Waves

They know their end is imminent,
even as they come into existence.
Temporary Himalayas,
chased relentlessly by time.

Until,
they run into the ultimate obstacle.
Humbled down,
into a carpet of millions of tingling, sparkling souls

Begging,

for their reincarnation

Mother

I was born in your abyss,
along with many other creatures.

We huddled in your translucent blanket,
sheltering in the darkness,
thriving in suspended incubation.

Oblivious to the threats outside,
we had you to protect us.
Always ready to become a martyr,
throw yourself on the rocks,
the crushing sound of your body our lullaby.

And we grew,
And we grew.
And when we reached the surface,
we forgot about you.

Abalone

At the bottom of the dark ocean,
You couldn't stop dreaming of the sky.

Luring rainbows down into your spiral staircase,
you trapped them one by one,
keeping them hostage in a fractal whirlpool.

Shimmering on your iridescent shell,
a thousand ancient sunsets,
replayed in high definition.

Bleeding hot turquoise on your canvas,
A thousand painted rivers,
merging into the sky,
interrupted by neon-purple lightning storms,
fading into lilac blossoms,
as you pivot in the current.

At the bottom of the ocean.

Graveyard

At the depths of the abyss
there is a grey layer of mud,
many miles thick.
It is where Earth keeps her diary.

Out of human reach,
in the dark,
this is where she records everything:
all the things that have happened
over billions of years:
from whales' bones,
to shipwrecks,
to plastic bottles.

She holds on to it all, lovingly,
like a mother crafting photo albums,
whether it was a good or a bad memory.

She carefully collects each piece,
caresses it in soft mud,
and keeps it in her arms forever.
A scrapbook of accomplishments,
by all her children:
the good ones,
and the other ones.

Black Morning

You will know the day has arrived,
when the wind can't clear the stench
of burning corpses,
as the mountains hide behind the smoke.

You will know it's here,
when the sun barely rises,
stuck midway over the horizon,
in a permanent brown sunset.

You will know it,
When the footsteps behind you quickly fill with blood,
as you walk on the beach.
When the waves begin to flow backwards,
running away from the land,
running away from you.

You will know it,
When the world becomes an endless morgue,
and you curl up in a fetal position,
waiting to be fossilised.

You will feel it,
that this is the day,
the day that you've been dreading all along

Reunion

Today the long-gone sister finally returns home.
Suffocated in her heavenly castle,
she turns herself into sad tears,
falling into the arms of her older sibling.

Separated at birth,
torn between Heaven and Earth,
they couldn't be more different.

Yet they are sisters from the same mother.
As each tear falls,
it turns into a heartbeat,
celebrating their eternal bond.

Because they both know they'll meet again:
without rain there is no sea,
without sea there is no rain.

Shipwrecked

Born out of chaos,
they dress up in liquid emeralds
and escape their turbulent home.

Half-way across the world,
they become aware of their own futility:
running away was never a solution,
the chaos was inside them all along,
following them on their journey.

Relentless fugitives exhausted from the chase,
they expire quietly on the beach.

a last breath,
a sigh,
a release.
A picture wiped clean

Mortal

Sometimes sinking,
other times barely floating,
I was baptized by near-drowning.

Yet it is in these,
unstable sediments,
where I have learned to thrive:
Trailing shifting shores,
winding paths over garlands of seashells,
forgotten carcasses and aborted urchins,

I hunt for the moments,
as the moments disappear,
like sand slips through fingers.

From deluge to sunstroke,
I try to imitate the life of a rock,
despite being made of flesh and blood.

I try to turn moments into lifetimes,
string them into necklaces,
and leave them on the shore,
before the next wave.

Oath

One look into the ocean wind suffices
to become hostage again,
to the grip of melancholy.

Like a misplaced photo album,
disowned memories re-emerge
of those blue-tinted, incandescent days,
when galloping lions hurried triumphantly towards the shore,
diffusing into mist.

They serve as a reminder
of how I came to be,
of that day when I stumbled down into the sharp rocks
where crimson rivulets made a promise to the storm
and I was baptized by accident,
adopted against my will,
infused forever with the sadness of the sea.

Since then I carry the storm
like a bottle haunted by its bittersweet elixir,
infused into my pores,
distilled back into the mist,
carried,
by the wind.

Printed in Great Britain
by Amazon